TEN TRUE
ANIMAL RESCUES

TEN TRUE
ANIMAL RESCUES

Jeanne Betancourt

A
LITTLE APPLE
PAPERBACK

SCHOLASTIC INC.
New York Toronto London Auckland Sydney

Cover illustration by Bill Dodge

ISBN 0-590-68117-6

12   2 3/0

Printed in the U.S.A.   40
First Scholastic printing, November 1998

CONTENTS

TEN TRUE
ANIMAL RESCUES

1

THREE-ALARM FIRE

The night of June 30, 1997, members of the Holman family were fast asleep in their redbrick house in Hamden, Connecticut. Mr. Holman was in the master bedroom downstairs. Mrs. Holman and twelve-year-old Caitlin were in Caitlin's room on the second floor. Meghan, seven, was in her bedroom across the hall.

Snowball, Meghan's buff–colored teddy bear hamster, was in his metal cage under the window in her room. When Meghan first got Snowball, she put him in a habitat equipped with plastic tubes. But the fluffy hamster sometimes got stuck in the tubes and had to be rescued. So the Holmans bought him a big metal cage. He would jump on the wooden seesaw, ride on the metal wheel, and skitter in and out of a little plastic house.

Around one o'clock in the morning, Meghan woke up to a strange screeching sound coming from Snowball's cage. He was pushing against the bars of the cage to make the screechy noises. At first, Meghan was annoyed with Snowball for waking her up. Then she noticed a strange light in the room and saw what was bothering him. Flames were darting out of the wall right next to Meghan's bed.

Meghan jumped out of bed and ran into her sister's room.

"There's a fire in my room!" Meghan

shouted to her sleeping mother and sister.

Mrs. Holman remembered that Meghan sometimes walked in her sleep. She thought her daughter was having a sleepwalking dream and told her to go back to bed.

"Flames are coming out of my wall," Meghan insisted.

Mrs. Holman decided to take Meghan back to her room to show her there wasn't a fire. But when Mrs. Holman walked into Meghan's room, she realized that Meghan hadn't been dreaming. Flames *were* shooting out of the wall right next to her daughter's bed.

"Go wake up your father!" Mrs. Holman shouted to Meghan and Caitlin. Meanwhile, she ran into the bathroom and grabbed a towel. She tried to put out the flames with the towel. As she was slapping at the flames she noticed an orange light behind the wall. The house was on fire behind the wall, too! She had to get her family out of there fast.

The whole family ran outside in their pajamas and bare feet. The family dog and cat raced out right behind them. Mr. Holman called the fire department on his cellular phone and the firefighters were soon there.

About ten minutes after they got out of the burning house, Meghan realized that they had left Snowball behind.

By then, flames and smoke filled the second story of the Holman house. Meghan's hamster was in her burning bedroom, and it was too late to save him.

After the fire was put out, the Holmans couldn't go back home. The second floor of the house was damaged by the flames, smoke, and water. It would take a long time to clean and repair it, so the Holmans rented a house in another town. They would live there until their house was repaired.

The Holmans told everyone how the hamster had warned them of the fire and probably saved Meghan's life. Meghan lost most of her belongings in the fire. Her clothes, toys, and books were all destroyed. But Meghan was saddest about losing her pet hamster. She couldn't forget Snowball. She wanted to bury him in the backyard, next to the grave of her hermit crab, Hermes.

Four days after the fire, Mr. Holman went into Meghan's damaged room to get Snowball's body for a family burial ceremony. He was shocked to find that Snowball's cage was empty. He figured that Snowball had escaped from his cage during or after the fire.

But where had Snowball gone? the Holmans wondered. Was he still *alive*?!

Mr. Holman looked all over the house, but didn't find the hamster.

A week passed and Snowball was still missing.

Everyone had a different theory about what had happened to Snowball. Some thought he had run away. Others said he had probably died someplace in the house. The one thing everyone agreed on was that they would never see Snowball again.

Eleven days after the fire, a carpenter, Jim Buller, was taking down a damaged wall in Meghan's room. As Jim looked into an opening in the floor, he was surprised to see two tiny eyes staring at him.

Jim poked a finger toward the creature. It bit him. Jim thought the animal was a rat. He looked closer and saw that it was much too fluffy for a rat. Then he realized it was a hamster — probably the hero hamster he had heard so much about.

Jim used hamster food and water to encourage Snowball to come out. Snowball was so thirsty he practically took a bath in the water. Next, Jim put Snowball and the food in the old hermit crab cage and called the Holmans to tell them the good news.

Snowball had a wonderful reunion with Meghan and the rest of the Holman family.

When I was interviewing Mrs. Holman about their heroic hamster, she told me how just that day Snowball had bumped downstairs inside his plastic ball toy. "He's always getting into trouble," Mrs. Holman told me, laughing.

That may be true. But one night in June 1997, Snowball got the Holmans *out of trouble* by warning them about a fire — a fire that was burning only two feet from Meghan Holman's bed.

2

A SNOWY GRAVE

Snow can be beautiful, and playing in it can be lots of fun. But snow and strong wind together can create a blizzard. And blizzards can be extremely dangerous. Andrea Anderson learned that lesson the hard way.

Eleven-year-old Andrea lived in a house near the ocean in a New Jersey town. It was snowing so hard when she woke up one morning in February that the schools were closed.

Andrea and her two sisters went out to play in the snow. The three girls threw snowballs at one another and dug tunnels in the hills of snow. After a while, Andrea's sisters said they were cold and went into the house, but Andrea stayed outside to play some more.

The snow swirled around Andrea in big gusts, and the temperature dropped. The fierce wind sent shivers through her body. She decided that it was too cold to have fun outside any longer. So, a few minutes after her sisters went in, Andrea headed toward the house.

The wind was picking up speed and power. Andrea tried to walk against the wind but kept losing ground. It drove the sixty-five-pound girl backward, away from her house and toward the sand dunes and the sea.

Suddenly, a gust of wind, like a big hand, pushed Andrea into a five-foot bank of snow. She was buried up to her chest. Trapped!

Andrea struggled to get out of the snow, but the more she struggled, the more the snow and wind held her down. Snow was falling on her even harder now, and her body was freezing cold.

Andrea shouted for help. Every time she opened her mouth, snow flew into it. The wind made her eyes water; tears froze on her cheeks. She could barely hear her own voice. The *whooshing* of the wind grew louder. She kept screaming anyway.

No human could hear Andrea because the wind was too loud. But an animal heard her cries. A neighbor's black Newfoundland puppy, Villa, was in her fenced-in dog run. Andrea lived next door to Villa's owners, the Viets. She often played with Villa and dog-sat when the Viets were away. Now, Villa pricked up her ears when she heard Andrea's high-pitched cries. She must have recognized Andrea's voice.

Villa listened carefully. Andrea's cry for help was coming from outside the five-foot fence. The fence was there to keep the year-old puppy in the yard. Villa had never tried to jump it, but she had to reach Andrea. She had to get to the other side of the fence.

The dog made a run to the high fence, leaped up, scrambled over the top, and dropped to the other side. She shook off the snow. The wind pushed hard against her. But she stood her ground, waiting to hear the cries again.

Andrea had no idea that help was on the way. Her throat hurt from screaming. She couldn't move her arms or legs. She was freezing cold and must have been terrified.

Andrea managed to yell for help one more time. Villa bounded toward the sound coming from the snowbank. She saw Andrea, reached her, and began licking her.

Villa's tongue warmed Andrea's freezing face. Then Villa moved around and around Andrea. She was using her 100-pound body to "shovel" away the snow. But Andrea still couldn't free herself.

After a few minutes, Villa stopped turning in circles and positioned her neck right in front of Andrea. Andrea put her arms around Villa's neck and held on tightly.

Villa began pulling and pulling.

Finally, Andrea felt the snow loosen around her legs. She was moving! Andrea pushed with her feet while Villa pulled. In a final push-pull, Andrea was free of the snowbank.

It was hard for Andrea to stand upright in the strong wind. Would she fall back into that snowy coffin that had held her prisoner?

Everywhere Andrea looked she saw swirling snow. She couldn't see any houses. She wasn't even sure which direction to go. She tried to step forward. It was impossible. The snow was too deep and the wind was too strong. Daylight was fading, and the gray sky was turning dark.

Villa put her head near Andrea's freezing hands. Andrea again grabbed hold of the fur on Villa's neck. The snowdrifts were higher than Villa, too. The dog nosed her way into the deep snow, wiggling her body at the same time. She was making a path to the house for both of them.

Andrea didn't know where Villa was going. She had to trust the strong black puppy because she was her only hope.

Andrea held Villa's neck tightly. Villa plowed the two of them through the high snow. It must have been hard to hold onto Villa's neck with all the snow and wind. If Andrea lost her hold on Villa, the dog would stop. Slowly, they inched forward.

Finally, Andrea could see the lights of a house through the cloud of falling snow. It was her house! Villa dragged Andrea up onto the porch. Then the clever dog scratched at the door.

Andrea's mother heard the scratching and opened the door. Mrs. Anderson found her shivering, sobbing daughter on the porch. She was shocked to learn that the storm had become so dangerous that her daughter had almost died in it.

The storm became known as the "Blizzard of '83." Some people in New Jersey say they'll never forget it.

Andrea Anderson certainly won't. And she'll never forget the young neighbor who saved her life.

Villa received two dog-hero awards for her rescue mission.

3

SHARK ATTACK!

Sharks are dangerous ocean companions. People don't usually go into the ocean when a shark is close by. That's an ocean-swimming safety rule that most people obey. Other swimming safety rules are:

• Go in only when the water is calm.

• Stay close to shore.

• Be sure a lifeguard is on duty where he or she can see you.

A woman broke all of those rules in Florida more than fifty years ago. She didn't plan to, but she did. People in Florida are

15

still talking about what happened to that lucky swimmer.

There were very few people on the beach that day in August 1943. And there was no lifeguard. But the surf seemed calm. The woman took off her sandals and waded into the ocean. Even though there wasn't a lifeguard nearby, she thought she was safe. The water was only up to her waist. She was obeying the first two safety rules. She wasn't far from the shore and the water was calm. But the surf wasn't really calm that day — it just looked like it was. There was actually a strong undertow.

In a split second, the undertow knocked the woman off her feet and dragged her under. She gulped big mouthfuls of ocean water. A rush of water went up her nose and down into her lungs.

The undertow flung her head over heels. As she tumbled around, she struggled to breathe. The water slapped against her and pulled her into deeper water.

The woman tried to swim in the rough waters, but she couldn't fight the undertow. She was being swept out farther and farther from the shore.

She wasn't the only one out in that deep water, however. A shark had spotted her and was headed in her direction.

The desperate woman's cries for help were too weak to be heard onshore.

A dolphin was swimming close by and noticed the woman. It also saw the deadly shark. Dolphins don't like sharks and often have fights with them. The dolphin didn't want that shark to attack the woman. If it did, there would be blood in the water. And blood would attract more sharks. Then the dolphin would be in great danger, too.

The dolphin headed toward the shark at full speed. Its big snout was aimed at the shark's gills. *BAM!* The dolphin struck the shark. Before the shark could turn and counterattack, the dolphin struck again. This time the injured shark turned away from the drowning woman.

The woman wasn't even trying to swim or breathe anymore. She was floating facedown in the water. She was probably unconscious.

But the dolphin didn't turn away from her. It swam under the drowning woman and lifted her up on its back. Now her face was out of the water. The dolphin caught a big wave and swam toward shore.

There was a man on the dunes who saw the dolphin. He couldn't believe his eyes. A dolphin was riding the waves toward shore with a lifeless woman draped over its back!

The dolphin couldn't come up on the shore with its passenger. It would be as dangerous for the dolphin to be on the sandy beach as it was for the woman to be in the deep water. So the dolphin turned sharply when it was close to the beach.

When it turned, the woman flew through the air and landed safely on the sand.

She found herself on her hands and knees, coughing and spitting out water. She was alive. Minutes before, she had been drowning in the ocean. A shark had been coming toward her. Now she was safe on the beach. She knew that her life had been saved by a stranger, and that the stranger must have been a strong swimmer to pull her out of those deep, rough waters.

When she caught her breath, she stood up and turned to thank the stranger. But no one was there. Where was the person who had rescued her?

The man on the dunes who had witnessed the dolphin's rescue ran across the beach toward the woman. When he reached her, he told her how the dolphin had saved her.

The woman and the man looked out to sea. They could see the dorsal fin of a large shark as it swam out to deeper waters. Right behind it was the leaping dolphin. It was herding the shark farther away from the shore.

The woman knew that the man was right. A dolphin had saved her life.

4

STOP!

Brian Long wanted a dog and saved up his own money to buy a puppy. The tenth-grader named her Athena after the Greek goddess of wisdom and spent as much time as he could with her. Brian took good care of Athena, but he had to take care of himself, too. Because he's a diabetic, Brian has to give himself an insulin shot every day. Without enough insulin (or sugar) in his body he could go into shock or a coma.

One morning, Brian was late for school. It was 7 A.M. and time to meet the school bus. He quickly stuck himself with a hypodermic needle and injected a dose of insulin. He hurried outside and found Athena was waiting for him. Brian hugged his big black puppy and the two of them walked down the long driveway.

When Brian got to the highway in front of the house, he sat down on the bank of a drainage culvert to wait for the bus. Seconds later he passed out and fell over into a ditch. Even though Brian had given himself the insulin shot, there still wasn't enough sugar in his body.

Athena tried to wake Brian with licks and whimpers. But Brian remained unconscious. He didn't know where he was or what was happening to him. There was nothing Brian could do to help himself.

Several cars drove by without noticing that Brian was in trouble. Even the school bus went by without stopping. Athena needed to do something to help Brian.

The dog left the boy's side and went out to the middle of the highway. She stood there defiantly waiting for a car to come by and stop. Cars did come by. They even slowed down when they saw a dog in the middle of the road. But they went around her and drove on. None of them stopped to find out why a puppy was facing them in the middle of the road. They didn't realize the seven-month-old dog was asking for help.

After a while a teacher, Sandra Hamilton, drove down the highway. She saw the dog. She also saw the boy lying facedown in a drainage ditch, but she didn't realize anything was wrong. So, like so many other cars that morning, she steered around the dog and kept driving.

But Sandra kept thinking about what she had just seen. She wondered why a boy was lying in a ditch. Was something wrong with him? Or maybe he was just looking for something. She had to find out if that boy was okay.

Sandra Hamilton turned her car around and drove back to where she'd seen the dog and the boy.

The dog was still in the middle of the road and the boy hadn't moved from the ditch. Sandra pulled her car up beside the boy. She yelled, "Are you all right?" Brian didn't respond. Something *is* wrong with that boy, thought Sandra.

Fortunately, Sandra knew the signs of insulin shock and she quickly realized that Brian might be suffering from it. She also knew that Brian might be in a coma. Sandra drove up the family's driveway, blaring the car horn. She needed help.

Brian's mother was home, but she had

been in a car accident and couldn't get out of bed. Luckily, Brian's sister and brother were also home. His sister answered the door. When Brian's brother, Kevin, heard that Brian was unconscious he immediately knew what to do. If it wasn't too late, giving him sugar could save his brother's life. Kevin grabbed some apple juice and ran out of the house. Sandra called an emergency number for help.

Kevin poured apple juice into Brian's mouth and Athena licked his face. By the time the ambulance arrived, Brian was waking up.

It was now 7:45 A.M. Brian had blacked out for almost forty-five minutes. If he had been unconscious much longer he could have died. Athena and Sandra saved his life.

Later, when Brian thought about the morning, he realized that he hadn't eaten much for breakfast. It is important for diabetics to always eat enough at meals and to take their insulin.

Brian learned two things that morning. One was how important it is for him to keep to his special diet. Insulin alone is not enough. The second lesson Brian learned is that he has a very special dog and friend in Athena. She acted quickly and bravely. She truly lived up to her namesake, the goddess of wisdom.

5

ON THE WILD SIDE

People enjoy visiting zoos and seeing animals. Zoos are carefully designed to keep the animals separated from their many visitors. Fences and other barriers keep both the visitors and the animals safe.

That's the way it is supposed to be.

But one August day in 1996, a little boy crossed the line. He went into the wild side.

The three-year-old child was visiting the Brookfield Zoo in Chicago with his mother. The boy suddenly ran ahead of his mother. Before anyone could stop the child, he climbed over the four-foot railing around the gorilla exhibit. Visitors to the zoo watched helplessly as the little boy dropped eighteen feet into the gorilla pit. His head hit the concrete floor with a thump. He lay motionless.

Seven gorillas lived in that part of the gorilla exhibit. They heard the thump and saw that something unusual had fallen into their territory. The gorillas were curious and wanted to investigate. They all moved toward the child.

The first gorilla to reach the boy was Binti — a mother gorilla with a baby gorilla on her back.

The 150-pound gorilla picked up the injured child. When the other gorillas came toward her, Binti turned away from them and held onto the child.

A few zookeepers were having lunch near one of the entrances to the gorilla exhibit. They saw Binti holding a human child who wasn't moving or making a sound.

Was the child dead or alive? They couldn't be sure.

Binti cradled the child in her arms.

The zookeepers wondered how they could safely take the child from Binti. They knew it was very important not to excite or frighten the big animal. She was strong and could easily hurt the boy, even without intending to.

The zookeepers were also afraid of what the other gorillas might do. Would they try to take the boy from Binti? Would they injure him even more?

Someone had the idea to spray water between Binti and the other gorillas. The other gorillas wouldn't cross the barrier of water, not even to get to the interesting object that Binti was holding. The zookeepers pointed a hose into the exhibit. A strong stream of water hit the floor and sprayed the air between Binti and the other gorillas.

Everyone watching the frightening scene wondered what would happen next. Binti was apparently taking good care of the child. But if the boy was still alive, he obviously needed medical attention quickly. The zookeepers had to find a way to take the child from Binti safely.

Suddenly, Binti turned toward the door to the gorilla exhibit. She walked to it, carrying the child in her arms.

The zookeepers on the other side of the door watched her nervously. What was Binti going to do with the child?

Then, to their amazement, Binti placed the child on the floor right next to the door. She placed him where the zookeepers could reach him.

The zookeepers opened the door and

lifted the child out of the habitat. An emergency medical crew was already there. They checked the child for signs of life.

He was breathing! He was still alive! The ambulance rushed him to a nearby hospital. The child had a serious head injury, but he recovered fully.

Had Binti known that the boy was injured and needed help? Is that why she put him where he could be taken care of by the humans? Or was she protecting the child from the other gorillas by giving him up? Maybe both. We'll never know. What we do know is that Binti took very good care of the child. She protected the little boy from the other gorillas and brought him to a safe place.

Binti is still at the Brookfield Zoo. She is the gorilla who rescued a child.

6

A CRY FOR HELP

Bernita and Roy Rogers wanted to have a baby. Their first three children had died while they were being born, but the Rogers still wanted to try to have a baby. When their fourth child was born, they were so happy. They named their little girl Stacey. She was a healthy, beautiful baby.

Bernita was a nurse and she watched baby Stacey closely. Stacey weighed only five pounds when she was six weeks old. Most babies weigh a lot more than that, but

Stacey was healthy at five pounds. To be extra sure Stacey was safe, the Rogerses put a baby monitor in the nursery. Bernita carried a receiver around the house. Whenever Stacey cried, Bernita could hear her.

The Rogerses' cat, Midnight, loved the newest member of the household. He would often sit by Stacey's crib and watch her. The cat would follow Bernita around when she carried the baby in her arms.

When Stacey was six weeks old, she came down with a bad cold. Bernita immediately brought Stacey to her doctor for a checkup.

The doctor examined Stacey. He told Bernita that Stacey had a common cold, and he suggested putting a humidifier in the baby's room to help her breathe. The doctor said that Stacey would be fine in a day or two.

Bernita was relieved that nothing was seriously wrong with Stacey. When she brought her baby home, Midnight scampered around excitedly. He followed the mother and daughter into the nursery.

Soon, Stacey fell asleep in her crib and Bernita went into the living room. Because the doctor had said Stacey was fine, Bernita could relax. She sat down to rest. She wasn't surprised when Midnight came into the living room. Midnight was a "people cat" and always stayed close to her, Roy, or Stacey. Bernita figured Midnight would settle down and rest a little, too.

She was wrong. The cat meowed loudly and batted at Bernita's legs. She told him to behave and let her relax.

But Midnight kept pestering Bernita. When Midnight still wouldn't settle down, Bernita shooed him away.

The black cat ran from the living room, and Bernita thought she'd finally have a much-needed rest.

Suddenly, she heard an eerie moaning sound. *It was coming over the baby monitor!*

Bernita ran to the nursery.

The first thing she saw was Midnight standing on the dresser, howling into the monitor.

She looked at her baby in the crib. Stacey's skin was turning blue. She was gasping for air. Stacey couldn't breathe. If she couldn't breathe, she would die. Stacey was in danger.

Bernita grabbed Stacey and rushed to the car. She had to get her baby to the emergency room as fast as possible.

Bernita must have wondered if she was going to lose her fourth baby. Would Stacey die on the way to the hospital?

In the emergency room, doctors feverishly worked on the infant. Within minutes, a doctor told Bernita and Roy that they were able to help Stacey breathe again. She had a viral infection in her lungs, but she would live. The doctor also told them that they had reached the hospital just in time. It was lucky that Bernita had discovered that her baby was having trouble breathing when she did.

Bernita remembered how the cat had raced around, meowed, and batted at her legs. Midnight had been trying to tell her that Stacey was in danger. Stacey couldn't cry because she couldn't breathe. So Midnight went into her room and cried into the monitor for her. He was Stacey's cry for help.

Midnight had saved Stacey's life.

Stacey and Midnight grew up together. When Stacey turned ten years old, Midnight was twelve, which is pretty old for a cat.

Midnight now spends most of his time lying in the sun. But he still follows Stacey around and sleeps at the foot of her bed.

7

UNDER THE ICE

People who live near lakes often walk on them in the winter. Of course, they have to wait until the lake has iced over enough. A frozen lake is a fine place for ice skating, ice hockey, and interesting winter walks. It's fun — unless the ice breaks and you fall into the freezing water.

The folks living around a small lake in Indiana knew that walking and playing on thin ice was dangerous. So neighbors gathered each winter to measure the ice. They agreed not to go on the ice until it was more than four inches thick. They knew ice that thick could hold their weight and would not break.

In the winter of 1995, the ice on the lake was more than four inches thick. People skated and walked on it without worry.

But in mid–February there were a few unusually warm days. The ice was melting. Unfortunately, twelve-year-old Josh Mitchell didn't think about what the warm weather would do to the ice on the lake. He was going to a friend's house across the lake from his own house. Cutting across the frozen lake was the shortest route.

Denise and George Hamand were a couple who lived near the lake. They knew that the ice was thinning, and they were careful not to walk on it. They kept their dog, Levi, from going out there, too.

The Hamands have a good view of the lake from their house. If they had seen Josh, they would have warned him not to walk on the thin ice.

Levi, who is a golden-and-Labrador-re-triever mix, *did* see the boy. Levi was sitting at a window and saw that Josh was in danger. Levi whimpered loudly.

George heard Levi's worried sounds and went to see what was wrong. He followed Levi's gaze out the window and saw Josh on the lake. Like Levi, he was concerned for the boy's safety. He had to warn Josh to turn back.

But before George could open a window and yell out his warning, the ice under Josh cracked. George and Levi watched helplessly as Josh fell into the ten-foot-deep frigid water. Josh was thrashing wildly to keep from sinking. If he did sink, he might drift under the ice and be trapped. He would drown for sure.

George yelled to Denise to get Levi's

twenty-foot-long leash. He planned to throw it to the boy. If Josh grabbed the leash, maybe they could pull him out.

George and Levi ran outside while Denise ran for the long leash.

George knew that the boy needed *something* to hold onto — and quickly.

"Levi, fetch!" George ordered.

Levi leaped onto the ice, bounded over to the struggling boy, and dove into the water.

Josh put his arms around Levi's neck and screamed for help.

By that time, Denise had reached the shore with the leash. George threw out the leash to the boy. The leash was too short!

Then Denise and George saw the boy lose his grip on Levi and sink under the water. A few seconds later, he reappeared and grabbed onto the dog again. The Hamands knew that Levi would hold the boy up as long as he could. But they didn't know how long that would be. Especially because the panicky boy kept losing his grip on Levi.

Denise decided to go to Josh. She weighed more than Josh, so the ice probably wouldn't hold her, either. But she weighed less than her husband and was a stronger swimmer than he was. She would go out on the ice and help Levi with the rescue.

Denise got on all fours and crawled out onto the ice, making her way carefully to the boy and the dog who was keeping him afloat.

She'd almost reached them when she heard the ice crack under her. She felt the ice give way, and in an instant she sank into the water. It was freezing, but Denise didn't think about that. Only four feet of ice separated her from Josh and Levi. She had to reach them.

"Hang on!" Denise yelled to Josh.

She kicked to stay afloat and pounded the hard surface of the ice with her fists and elbows. While she struggled to break the ice, Josh again lost his grip on Levi and disappeared under the water. Was he going farther under the ice where she wouldn't be able to reach him?

Denise kept hitting the ice until she broke through to where Levi swam and the boy had sunk.

But where was Josh? Denise couldn't see him. Had he already drifted under the ice?

Keeping her head above water, Denise felt all around underneath the ice. Finally, her hand touched a piece of clothing. She yanked and pulled. Josh came up. He was terrified and gasping for air. The panicked boy thrashed around. It was hard for Denise to keep both herself and Josh from drowning.

She flipped Josh over onto his back and told him, "Calm down. I know this is scary, but we're going to get out of here."

Meanwhile, George called Levi back to shore. The dog climbed out of the water and ran obediently to his master.

Two other people had joined George on the shore. One of them brought an extension ladder. They pushed the ladder out to the hole where Denise and Josh were floundering. But the ladder was only ten feet long and didn't reach them. George and the others stamped through the ice and stood waist-deep in the freezing water. They pushed the ladder out farther. Denise could now reach it.

She grabbed the closest rung of the ladder. First, she pushed Josh out of the hole in the ice. Then she climbed out herself.

Josh and Denise crawled carefully over the ice. With every move they were afraid the ice would give and they'd be back in the water. But the ladder distributed their weight, so they didn't fall in.

Denise and Josh made it safely to shore. By then, paramedics were there to bundle them in blankets, get them into an ambulance, and take them to the hospital. Denise fainted on shore and didn't wake up until she was in the hospital. Later, after Denise and Josh warmed up and did breathing exercises for their lungs, they were able to go home. The paramedics checked Levi, too. He was still cold but in good health.

Levi was a hero. He had warned George and Denise that Josh was on thin ice. Then he went out and stayed in the water with Josh so the boy would have something to hold onto.

Before the accident, Josh Mitchell hadn't known Levi, George, or Denise. After the accident they all became friends. Josh and his parents sent the Hamands a big bouquet of flowers, bones for Levi, and a gift certificate from a local pet shop.

Josh visits Levi regularly and plays with his four-legged neighbor and rescuer. But they stay off the frozen lake.

8

CRUSHED!

Donald Motram was riding his motorbike across his fields in Wales. The cattle farms there have large grassy fields on rolling hills. Donald's farm was so big that he motor-biked to check on his herd. He would look for a missing calf or cow or bring medicine to a sick cow. The cows were used to seeing Donald on his bike. They had heard the *putt-putt* of the motor before.

When Donald whizzed past his herd, one of the biggest cows, Daisy, would look up first. The bell around her neck clanged.

Daisy was the leader of all the cows. As the "bell cow," Daisy saved Donald a lot of work. When he called the cows to come in at night, she led them to the barn. They always obeyed her.

One August day in 1996, Donald had a job to do that Daisy couldn't do for him. There was a sick calf somewhere on his property. He had to find the calf and give it some medicine.

Because he was thinking about the sick calf, Donald had forgotten that there was a big bull staying on his ranch. And the bull was thinking about Donald.

The bull wasn't used to motorbikes. When he heard the loud noise of the motorbike, he looked up. His nostrils flared and his back hooves kicked the ground. He was ready to attack the loud, fast-moving motorbike. The bull charged across the field. He came toward Donald from behind. Donald couldn't see the bull coming at him, and he didn't hear him because of the bike's noisy motor.

CRASH!

Donald felt a strong thump on his back. He didn't know what had hit him. Donald fell to the ground and landed faceup. Now he knew what had hit him! A 3,300-pound bull was standing over Donald. The bull's eyes were angry and Donald could feel the bull's hot breath on his face. Then the bull began stamping on his chest and shoulders, butting Donald's legs with his horns. Sharp pains shot through Donald's body. He was going to be crushed or gored to death!

Donald screamed in pain and terror. He thought for sure that he was going to die. Then he blacked out.

Daisy heard Donald's screams. She looked up and saw the bull snorting and stamping on Donald. She mooed and ran toward the bull, her bell clanging loudly as she ran.

The other cows looked up from their grazing. If Daisy was going someplace, they knew they should follow her. The cows ran to catch up with Daisy. In seconds, the whole herd reached the bull and Donald.

Daisy threw her body against the bull. Then some of the other cows mooed loudly and pushed against the bull.

On the ground, Donald started to wake up. He wondered why his body hurt so much. It hurt to breathe. His mouth hurt, and he couldn't open it. Something was wrong with his jaw.

Then Donald remembered. The bull had almost trampled him to death. He tried to move so he could get away from the bull. But he couldn't. His pains and injuries would not let him.

Donald could hear the bull's snorts. He

looked around in terror. But this time, he didn't see the bull's angry eyes. Instead, he saw Daisy's gentle eyes. And next to her was another peaceful cow face. And another. And another. There was a whole circle of friendly cows surrounding him.

Nearby, the bull was still snorting and stamping on the ground. But he was outside the cow circle, and Daisy wouldn't let him in. Donald realized that his cows were protecting him.

The bull made a charge at the cows. He was madder than ever. He wanted to stamp on Donald some more. But the cows wouldn't budge, especially Daisy. She held her ground, and so did the others.

Every breath Donald took sent sharp pains across his chest. The bull had cracked his ribs. And he couldn't scream because his jaw was broken. Donald knew that he was still in danger. The bull was much bigger than Daisy. Would Daisy and the other cows give up? Would the bull come back and attack again? All he could do was lie there and wait.

Donald waited and prayed. After a while, he didn't hear the bull snorting anymore. He even thought he heard the bull run away. Had the animal finally given up? Or was he *pretending* to give up?

Donald lifted his head and looked around. The bull was gone. But the cows had not moved. They wouldn't leave him unprotected.

Donald managed to turn himself over. Then he started to crawl. Every movement sent sharp, stinging pains through his body. He crawled very slowly. The circle of cows, led by Daisy, moved with him. They were his bodyguards. His convoy. His protectors.

Donald pulled himself along the ground.

It hurt to open his mouth, but he still managed to groan for help.

Finally, someone at the ranch heard his groans.

Finally, Donald Motram was safe.

It took Donald more than five months to recover from his wounds. But he was alive — thanks to Daisy.

Daisy is still the "bell cow" on Donald's farm. And she will always be Donald's hero.

9

INJURED KING

On December 26, 1981, Fern and Howard Carlson, their sixteen-year-old daughter, Pearl, and their dog, King, were all sleeping. Mr. and Mrs. Carlson were in their bedroom, and Pearl was in hers. King, a German shepherd mix, was asleep on the family room floor. The sliding glass doors in the family room were left open so that King could go out whenever he wanted.

The house was peaceful, but it didn't stay that way for long.

The ·smell of smoke woke King. The

smoke was seeping under the door separating the family room from the utility room. King could have run through the open doors in the family room to the outside, but he didn't. He wanted to get to the Carlsons and warn them about the fire.

King ran first to the utility room, the source of all the smoke. The utility room door was closed. But going through that room was the only way for King to reach his owners. How could he break through it?

King's sharp claws, powerful teeth, and jaws were his only tools. The brave dog clawed and chewed at the hot door. Splinters pierced his jaw and the heat burned his paws, but still he worked at the door. Finally, he made a hole.

King pushed his body into the hole. Splintered wood cut his flesh, smoke filled his lungs, and flames darted at him. He pushed on until he was through the door and inside the burning room.

Fearlessly, he charged through the hot, smoky room into the hall. But flames filled the hall and blocked the doorway to the Carlsons' bedrooms.

King tried to go through the flames. They singed his fur and forced him back. Then King noticed an opening in the flames and jumped through it. He found his way to Pearl's room.

Pearl was sound asleep. King whined and poked at the girl until she woke up. Smoke was filling the house. Pearl realized instantly that the house was on fire. She had to warn her parents.

Pearl and King couldn't go through the hallway, because it was an inferno. Pearl remembered that there was another doorway to her parents' bedroom. The way was smoky, but there weren't any flames. They took that path to her parents' bedroom.

Pearl ran over to the bed and woke her mother. Smoke burned Mrs. Carlson's eyes and filled her lungs. She yelled to her husband that they had to get out.

Pearl and her mother then ran to the window and crawled through it to safety. They thought Mr. Carlson was following them and yelled for King to come, too.

But Mr. Carlson couldn't follow his family to safety. He was still in bed. He had a lung condition and was choking on the smoke. When he did manage to stumble out of bed he went in the wrong direction. Then, overcome by the smoke, he fell to the floor, unconscious.

King ran to the open window. But he didn't go out to the cool fresh air and safety. When Mrs. Carlson saw King at the window, she realized that her husband hadn't followed her. She knew King would not leave the burning building without Mr. Carlson.

Mrs. Carlson climbed back into the smoky room, and King led her through the heat and smoke to her unconscious husband.

She bent over her husband, revived him, and helped him up. Mr. Carlson put an arm around his wife's shoulder and held onto King's fur with his other hand. Together, Mrs. Carlson and King led Mr. Carlson to the window. The Carlson family was safe.

Big and little splinters had to be pulled from King's jaw. He had a bad cut on his neck, but he recovered fully.

On Christmas Eve, five years before the fire, the Carlsons had found King on their doorstep. He was starving and badly injured from a gunshot wound. That Christmas the

Carlsons took King into their home and hearts. They saved his life.

Five years later, King repaid the Carlsons by saving *their* lives. It was a Christmas present none of them would ever forget.

10

LOST AT SEA

Many people work at sea and depend on sturdy boats to keep them safe out on the water. But sometimes the wind, rain, and raging seas are stronger than the boats. Then lives are in danger.

In 1930, off the coast of the state of Washington, a tugboat named *Barney Jr.* lost a battle with a stormy sea. There were two men on the *Barney Jr.* that day — Arthur Clayton, a radio operator, and the ship's cook, C. H. Coulson. The *Barney Jr.* had a small lifeboat on board. But the men knew that if the big tug couldn't stay afloat, the little dinghy couldn't make it, either. The boat rocked so hard that it almost turned upside down. There wasn't any way that Arthur and C. H. could save themselves. They needed help. Fast.

Arthur sent out an S. O. S. signal. But he didn't think anyone could reach them in time to save them.

The boat was on its side. The wall of the cabin was where the floor used to be. Arthur had to crawl along the wall to get out on deck.

Arthur and C. H. both knew that the tugboat would soon roll over completely and sink, like a miniature *Titanic*.

Meanwhile, Albert Smith was scanning the stormy sea from a hill near the shore. He soon spotted the foundering boat and its helpless two-man crew. Albert wanted to rescue whoever was on that boat. But there was so little time and he was alone. Who could help him save the men?

Albert's only companion that day was his little saddle pony, Shotgun. Together, maybe they could save the men on the sinking boat. They had to try.

Albert mounted Shotgun and headed to the beach. As they galloped along the sand, Albert lost sight of the boat. Then he saw it again, tipped halfway over. The men were holding onto the bow and shouting for help. The sinking boat was a quarter-mile out, but the waters were too rough for swimming. Albert thought maybe a pony could swim through the surging sea. And maybe a man could stay on its back while it swam.

Arthur let the reins go slack and told Shotgun to go into the water.

Shotgun galloped into the foamy surf.

The wind and rain pelted rider and pony. Shotgun struggled against the wind to move forward in the freezing waters. For fifteen minutes, the pony strained to swim toward the sinking boat and its desperate crew.

Finally, the pony and her rider reached the men.

Arthur and C. H. couldn't believe their eyes. A pony had come to rescue them. But what could a pony do?

Albert Smith yelled to the men clinging to the tug. He told them to lower the lifeboat and Shotgun would pull it to shore.

The two men crawled over to the dinghy and let it drop into the sea. They climbed in and tied one end of a rope to the bow and threw the other end to Albert. He tied it to Shotgun's saddle horn.

Albert gave Shotgun the signal, and the

little pony headed toward shore. With a tremendous effort she pulled the dinghy that tossed on the waves.

As Shotgun struggled with her burden, the *Barney Jr.* rolled over. Shotgun and Albert had reached the men just in time. But could Shotgun pull the dinghy and its passengers safely to shore? Would they make it to solid ground?

Waves crashed over Shotgun, but she pushed on. Finally, her hooves touched the sandy bottom. Now, if they could only make it through the crashing, swirling waters.

The brave little pony seemed to be succeeding. A few more steps and the three men and Shotgun would reach shore safely.

Just then, Shotgun stepped into a deep hole and became caught in the twisting tide. A long, swirling wave pushed Albert out of the saddle and dragged him back out to sea. Meanwhile, the whirlpool yanked and twisted Shotgun around.

The men on the bouncing, storm-swept dinghy watched helplessly. They couldn't help Albert, Shotgun, or themselves. If they got out of the dinghy, they would be swept away by the ocean. Just like Albert. Their only hope was Shotgun.

Shotgun and the dinghy were at the mercy of the whirlpool. But Shotgun didn't give up. She struggled against the churning water until she found her footing. Her rider was no longer there to tell her what to do, but the dinghy was still tied to her saddle. Shotgun strained and pulled the dinghy, inch by inch, toward the beach.

Finally, the dinghy was on solid ground. The two men were safe.

But what about Albert? The men and pony looked out at the roiling sea. They couldn't see him.

Albert had to save himself. Water filled his lungs. The undertow was pulling him out deeper. He struggled and swam with all his strength. Finally, he made it to land, too.

The three men were safe.

And Shotgun was a hero.

Dear Reader:

I have three pets, an old dog named Willie and two young cats — Lucca and Todi. The animals I write about in this book performed heroic deeds by saving lives. Willie, Lucca, and Todi haven't saved me in any big way. But they make my life better and happier every day.

We are lucky to share our planet with other animals. Animals who make our lives richer and more fun. Animals who save our lives in big and little ways.

I hope you enjoy your pets as much as I do mine.

Happy reading. Happy writing. And have good times with your pets — big and small.

Jeanne Betancourt

ABOUT THE AUTHOR

Jeanne Betancourt is the author of the *Pony Pal* series. She has also written fifteen other books for children and young adults, including *Kate's Turn* and *My Name is ~~Brain~~ Brian*.

Pony Pals®

Be a Pony Pal®!

Free pony bookmark and collecting cards in every book

❏ BBC48583-0	#1	I Want a Pony	....	$2.99
❏ BBC48584-9	#2	A Pony for Keeps	....	$2.99
❏ BBC48585-7	#3	A Pony in Trouble	....	$2.99
❏ BBC48586-5	#4	Give Me Back My Pony	....	$2.99
❏ BBC25244-5	#5	Pony to the Rescue	....	$2.99
❏ BBC25245-3	#6	Too Many Ponies	....	$2.99
❏ BBC54338-5	#7	Runaway Pony	....	$2.99
❏ BBC54339-3	#8	Good-bye Pony	....	$2.99
❏ BBC62974-3	#9	The Wild Pony	....	$2.99
❏ BBC62975-1	#10	Don't Hurt My Pony	....	$2.99
❏ BBC86597-8	#11	Circus Pony	....	$2.99
❏ BBC86598-6	#12	Keep Out, Pony!	....	$2.99
❏ BBC86600-1	#13	The Girl Who Hated Ponies	.....	$2.99
❏ BBC86601-X	#14	Pony-Sitters	....	$3.50
❏ BBC86632-X	#15	The Blind Pony	....	$3.50
❏ BBC37459-1	#16	The Missing Pony Pal	....	$3.50
❏ BBC37460-5	#17	Detective Pony	....	$3.50
❏ BBC74210-8		Pony Pals Super Special #1: The Baby Pony	......	$5.99
❏ BBC86631-1		Pony Pals Super Special #2: The Lives of Our Ponies	.	$5.99
❏ BBC37461-3		Pony Pals Super Special #3: The Ghost Pony	......	$5.99

Available wherever you buy books, or use this order form.

Send orders to Scholastic Inc., P.O. Box 7500, Jefferson City, MO 65102

Please send me the books I have checked above. I am enclosing $_____ (please add $2.00 to cover shipping and handling). Send check or money order — no cash or C.O.D.s please.

Please allow four to six weeks for delivery. Offer good in the U.S.A. only. Sorry, mail orders are not available to residents in Canada. Prices subject to change.

Name_____ Birthdate ____/____/____

First   Last   M   D   Y

Address_____

City_____ State_____ Zip_____

Telephone (   )_____ ❏ Boy   ❏ Girl

Where did you buy this book?   ❏ Bookstore   ❏ Book Fair   ❏ Book Club   ❏ Other